# countdown to the First Day of school

**Third Edition**

A K-12 Get Ready Checklist for:

✓ Beginning Teachers

✓ Teacher Transfers

✓ Student/Preservice Teachers

✓ Mentors and School Administrators

✓ Teacher Educators

# NEA CHECKLIST SERIES
## an NEA Professional Library Publication

Leo M. Schell
Paul R. Burden

Copyright © 2006
National Education Association of the United States

Printing History:
First Printing: June 2000
Second Printing: August 2002
Third Printing: June 2006
Fourth Printing: September 2008

Note: The opinions in this publication should not be construed as representing the policy or position of the National Education Association. Materials published by the NEA Professional Library are intended to be discussion documents for educators who are concerned with specialized interests of the profession.

**Library of Congress Cataloging-in-Publication Data**
Schell, Leo M.

Countdown to the first day of school: a K-12 get-ready checklist for beginning teachers, transfer teachers, school administrators and mentors, teacher educators, student/preservice teachers / by Leo M. Schell, Paul R. Burden.—3rd ed.

p.cm. — (NEA checklist series)

Includes bibliographical references (p. )

ISBN 0-8106-2162-2

1. First year teachers—In-service training—United States—Handbooks, manuals, etc. 2. Teacher orientation—United States—Handbooks, manuals, etc. 3. Mentoring in education—United States—Handbooks, manuals, etc. 4. School management and organization—United States—Handbooks, manuals, etc. I. Burden, Paul R.   II. Title.   III. Series.

LB2844.1.N4 S34 2000
371.1—dc21

00-041579

# Contents

**5** About the Authors
**7** Introduction

## Getting Acquainted

**13** Instructional Resources
**14** Community Facilities and Resources
**15** The School District
**16** School Rules, Procedures, and Policies
**18** School Personnel, Services, and Facilities
**20** Your Classroom
**20** Your Students

## Making Management Preparations

**25** Organizing Materials
**25** Classroom Helpers
**26** Class Lists and Rosters
**27** School-Home Communication
**28** Birthdays and Other Celebrations
**29** Use of Instructional Resources

## Determining Procedures and Rules

**33** Classroom Procedures
**34** Rules

## Making Instructional Preparations

**39** Weekly Time Schedules
**39** Long-Range Plans
**43** Motivating Your Students
**43** Preparing for Lesson Planning
**44** Daily Lesson Plans

**45** Preparing a Syllabus and Policy Sheets
**45** Tentative Student Assessment
**46** Determining Your Grading Policy
**47** Planning for Homework
**49** Back-Up Activities
**49** Opening Class Routine
**49** Folder for Substitute Teachers

## Planning for the First Day
**53** Planning the First Day
**54** Conducting the First Day

## Organizing Your Classroom and Materials
**59** Room Identification
**59** Desk Arrangements
**59** Seat Selection and Name Tags
**60** Room Arrangement
**60** Room Decoration

## The Final Check
**65** Have These Materials Ready
**66** Final Check!
**67** Bibliography for Classroom Management and Related Issues

# About the Authors

**Leo M. Schell** is Professor Emeritus at Kansas State University in Manhattan, Kansas, where he taught for 31 years. A specialist in reading instruction, he published three books and numerous articles on the topic. Late in his professorial career, he immersed himself in the supervision of field experiences and of student teaching. Some results of this immersion were several published articles, numerous conference presentations, and two monographs on this topic.

**Paul R. Burden** is a professor and an assistant dean in the College of Education at Kansas State University, Manhattan, Kansas, where he has supervised student teachers and taught courses on classroom management and discipline, teaching methods, and instructional leadership. Previously, he was a middle-level science teacher. His other books include: *Methods for Effective Teaching* (2007, Allyn & Bacon), *Classroom Management: Creating a K-12 Learning Community* (2006, John Wiley & Sons), *Powerful Classroom Management Strategies: Motivating Students to Learn (2000, Corwin Press),* and *Establishing Career Ladders in Teaching* (1987, Charles C. Thomas). He can be reached at (785) 532-5550 or at burden@ksu.edu.

# Introduction

Beginning teachers are faced with a variety of professional challenges, particularly during the first few days of school. They are expected to enter the classroom equipped with (1) a thorough familiarity with the school's facilities, personnel, and policies and procedures; (2) a classroom management system that includes ways to prevent and to address student misbehavior; (3) a fair and an efficient system for student assessment; and (4) long-range and short-range instructional plans that meet curriculum standards and acknowledge students' varied abilities, interests, and backgrounds.

These are intimidating, yet mandatory, expectations. Research shows that, to a great degree, classroom organization and management during the first few days of school determine much of the instruction and social interaction that will persist throughout the school year.

Much of the instructional and social interaction that occurs throughout the school year can be traced directly or indirectly to the way teachers initially establish instructional and social systems during the first days of school. Because these first few days are so important, new teachers should engage in extensive planning and decision making before school starts.

# Why and How Was This Checklist Prepared?

Some school districts have tried to help new teachers: become familiar with school rules and procedures, facilities, and resources; plan for instruction; select instructional strategies; and manage student behavior. To achieve these goals, school districts have offered induction programs such as orientation workshops at the start of the year for all beginning teachers, and mentoring programs.

Unfortunately, many school districts lack the necessary resources needed to implement effective induction programs. In an effort to develop a resource for these districts and for beginning teachers, we surveyed 300 experienced teachers in a wide variety of districts throughout Kansas and asked them to list the crucial things an inexperienced teacher should do before the first day of school. Their suggestions were the basis for the content of the first edition of this booklet.

As we prepared this third edition, we wanted to provide guidance for K-12 teachers and their administrators. Therefore, we had a number of K-12 teachers critique the second edition and offer suggestions for improvement. In addition, we consulted the research literature on beginning teachers. As a result, the content in this checklist is organized into six categories: (1) Getting Acquainted; (2) Making Management Preparations; (3) Determining Procedures and Rules; (4) Making Instructional Preparations; (5) Planning for the First Day; and (6) Organizing Your Classroom and Materials. We have also included an annotated bibliography for those who would like to strengthen their knowledge in several important areas of concern for beginners.

# Who Can Benefit from This Checklist?

Even though this get-ready checklist was created primarily for beginning teachers, the content can be used by transfer teachers, school administrators and mentors, college professors responsible for training new teachers, and student teachers and other preservice teachers.

## *Beginning Teachers*

This get-ready checklist is designed, first and foremost, to help beginning teachers thoroughly prepare themselves for their new jobs. Most of the topics can be addressed in the weeks before school starts.

## Teacher Transfers

Teacher transfers who are about to enter a new learning environment will find that many of the checklist preparations will make their transition smoother. The section on getting acquainted with the community, district, and school should be particularly helpful.

## School Administrators and Mentors

School administrators and mentors will find this booklet helpful in their efforts to orient and guide new teachers. *Administrators should sit down with new teachers, review some of the most essential tasks, and see that the teachers have adequately planned for them.* Likewise, mentors or experienced teachers should help beginning teachers with these tasks. For example, they could help new teachers:

- Formulate a daily and weekly schedule.
- Determine the capabilities of specific children and the class as a whole, and discuss how these capabilities might relate to instruction.
- Develop long-range plans and skeleton plans, and suggest possible learning activities or resources in the school or community that fit into these plans.
- Arrange specific opportunities for new teachers to see other personnel in working and non-working situations.
- Develop a student assessment system.

## Teacher Educators

Teacher educators could use the information contained in this checklist as the basis for revising their course content and field experiences. For example, field experiences could be broadened to show students how to become acquainted with the school, the district, and the community and also how to prepare for substitute teachers as well as that exhilarating, nerve-racking first day of teaching on their own. All of these areas are covered in the get-ready checklist.

# When Should This Checklist Be Used?

A new teacher could use this checklist over a number of weeks before the start of school. The content in the checklist is sequenced in the general order in which the issues should be addressed, although individual variation is possible.

# How Should This Checklist Be Used?

All users should first read the table of contents and then rapidly read through the handbook to get a feel for its contents and potential uses. Then users may begin to implement individual sections.

The individual sections of this handbook can be worked on in any sequence depending upon the individual user. As each item is completed, it should be checked so yet-to-be completed items are evident.

# GETTING ACQUAINTED

**Y**our first step in preparing for the school year is to become thoroughly familiar with your new teaching environment. This environment includes (1) instructional resources; (2) community facilities and resources; (3) the school district; (4) school rules, procedures, and policies; (5) school personnel, services, and facilities; (6) your classroom; and (7) your students.

The more knowledgeable you are about each of these areas, the more confident you will feel about your job and the less time you'll need to devote to these areas during the first few weeks of school when time is at a premium.

Check ✓
when
completed

# Instructional Resources

☐ **1** Learn about school district and/or school philosophy, goals, or outcomes and think about how they may influence your teaching and the type of instructional materials you use.

☐ **2** Obtain and study student textbooks and workbooks and/or teacher's guides to determine:
- ▶ Basic instructional goals
- ▶ Subject matter to be taught
- ▶ Scope and sequence of skills to be taught
- ▶ Possible instructional strategies and learning activities
- ▶ Available tests or other assessment instruments
- ▶ Breadth of instruction—remedial, enrichment, review
- ▶ Possible overlap with or integration of curricular areas
- ▶ The relationship to mandatory district/state assessments.

☐ **3** Ask whether there are school, district, or state curriculum guides that pertain to you. Examine them to learn:
- ▶ General instructional goals
- ▶ Instructional topics
- ▶ Scope and sequence of skills to be taught
- ▶ Suggested instructional activities
- ▶ Their relationship to goals of professional organizations

☐ **4** Learn what supplementary resources are available at school, such as:
- ▶ Supplementary aids that accompany textbooks
- ▶ Library and/or media resources
- ▶ Technology (hardware and software)
- ▶ Web sites, Internet sources

*check ✓ when completed*

- ▶ Math manipulatives
- ▶ Lab equipment and supplies

☐ **5** Many states have mandated assessments. Learn about the format and content of these tests so your instruction can correspond to them.

☐ **6** Learn about any distance-learning opportunities, advanced placement classes, and alternative education opportunities that might be available to your students.

☐ **7** Ask about any special or experimental programs that you *must* or may incorporate into instructional time. These may include programs such as career education, economic education, and technology skills.

☐ **8** Find out how to order extra supplies and instructional materials.

# Community Facilities and Resources

☐ **1** Investigate resource facilities in the community that can enrich your students' learning experiences. Many communities have more than you might expect. Ask fellow teachers, administrators, parents, and neighbors about appropriate community resources to tap. Look for:

- ▶ Museums, historic sites, libraries, government agecies, and businesses.
- ▶ Places of business that could give tours, such as banks, post offices, dairies, restaurants, pet stores, airports, lumber yards, grocery stores, department stores, and newspaper plants.
- ▶ Local colleges or universities that provide lectures, performances, or facilities.
- ▶ Organizations such as a local historical society, Chamber of Commerce, and Audobon Society.

☐ **2** Ask fellow teachers, administrators, parents, and neighbors for suggestions about people in the community who can provide services to supplement your instruction. These resource people may include:

- People such as county-extension agents, mechanics, accountants, florists, salespersons, equipment operators, meteorologists, veterinarians, law-enforcement officers, local artists and craftspersons, attorneys, politicians/legislators, and bankers.

☐ **3** Match potential classroom visitors and field trips with major curricular topics.

# The School District

☐ **1** Ask for a map of the school district. You may want to drive through the neighborhoods of the school district.

☐ **2** Learn about:

- The amount and range of cultural, ethnic, and linguistic diversity
- The range of socioeconomic levels within the district
- Degree of transiency in the community
- Charter, private, magnet and/or parochial schools; who attends these schools and how this affects your enrollment

☐ **3** Find out how much time the students spend on a bus coming to school. This may help you estimate how early they have to get up, how early they should go to bed, or what chores or responsibilities they have before they get to school.

check ✓ when completed

# School Rules, Procedures, and Policies

Much of the information in this section may be included in an orientation meeting for new teachers or in a school or district handbook. If so, become thoroughly acquainted with it.

☐ **1** Learn about personnel policies that relate to you, such as sick days, personal leave, staff development plans, paycheck dates, and health insurance.

☐ **2** Learn exactly what your responsibilities and duties are concerning:
- Playground duty
- Lunchroom duty
- Hall-monitor duty
- Bus loading/unloading
- Open houses
- PTA/PTO meetings
- Committee membership
- Extracurricular activities, such as clubs, organizations, and athletics
- School assemblies
- Planning time
- Parent/teacher conferences

☐ **3** Know school procedures and policies that concern the actions of the students, such as:
- Hall passes
- Tardies
- Student absences and attendance
- Students who arrive early in the morning
- Student illness or injury during school
- Dismissal procedures
- Fire, earthquake, and tornado drills
- Bomb threats

Check ✓ when completed

- Security guards/officers, metal detectors, and security cameras
- Discipline—what is prohibited, what is permissible, and under what conditions
- Administration of medication
- Rules for the restroom, lunchroom, playground, and school bus
- Dress code
- Cell phones, pagers, MP3s, iPods, and handheld video games
- Laptop computers

☐ **4** Learn about school procedures and policies that directly concern you and your teaching, such as:

- Teacher aides and classroom volunteers
- Faculty and departmental meetings
- Scheduled evaluation observations by administrators
- Chain of command to follow in case of complaint
- Discretionary money for instructional purposes
- Staff development programs
- Mandated testing (the kind of tests and dates)
- Documentation of classroom incidents
- Lesson plan requirements
- Student records to be kept and forms to be filed
- Reservation and check-out procedures for instructional media
- Computer availability and use
- Email

check ✓ when completed

# School Personnel, Services, and Facilities

☐ **1** Request a mentor teacher or the name of an experienced teacher who can answer some of your questions and assist you both before school starts and throughout the year. *Asking for help, ideas, or affirmation indicates professionalism, not weakness.*

☐ **2** Learn about administrative, teaching, and support personnel within the school and the services they provide, such as:

- Principal and Assistant Principal
- Grade-level or subject-matter colleagues
- Librarian/media center director
- Computer lab technician
- Paraeducators/teacher aides
- Nurse
- Secretaries
- Custodians
- Security officers
- Teachers' union representative
- School psychologist
- Social worker
- Reading-resource teacher
- School counselors
- International language intereptors
- Speech therapist
- Special education teacher
- Gifted student facilitator
- Vocal/instrumental music teachers
- Art teacher

☐ **3** Learn about special school services for students from low-income families such as the following:

- Breakfast and lunch programs
- Medical or dental help

Check ✓
when
completed

- ▶ Clothing distribution
- ▶ After-school tutoring programs

☐ **4** Become acquainted with the school buildings, equipment, and grounds, such as:
- ▶ School office
- ▶ Faculty parking lot
- ▶ Teachers' lounge
- ▶ Photocopy and computer facilities
- ▶ Cafeteria
- ▶ Media center
- ▶ Health clinic
- ▶ Rooms for special classes—music, remedial reading, speech therapy, computer instruction, and so on
- ▶ Playground/recess areas
- ▶ Fire alarms and extinguishers
- ▶ Emergency exits

☐ **5** Learn about your school's status with the federal government's No Child Left Behind Act (NCLB).
- ▶ Are there curricular areas you are responsible for that will require extra attention in order to assure adequate yearly progress (AYP)?
- ▶ Learn about special programs or efforts to assure AYP that will affect you.
- ▶ Learn when last spring's assessment data will be available. Plan to make time in your long-range planning schedule to review the data and consider implications for your instruction.
- ▶ Learn the dates of the state assessments and include them in your long-range plan.

check ✓ when completed

# Your Classroom

☐ **1** Determine the number of assigned students.

☐ **2** Examine, organize, and inventory all school-issued textbooks, supplementary instructional materials, and school supplies.

☐ **3** Note desk styles (yours and students') as well as bookcases, display tables, and special equipment such as computers. (Actual room arrangement comes later; see page 60.)

☐ **4** Determine whether colleagues have resources you don't have but which you may share.

☐ **5** Practice using any computers in your room, including successfully running any software you and/or students may later use.

☐ **6** Ask whether you have any discretionary money with which to purchase other supplementary materials. If so, acquire some quality materials by:

> ▶ Checking school supply catalogs that your school has on hand
>
> ▶ Visiting a local teacher supply store.

# Your Students

☐ **1** Learn as much as possible about your students, individually, as a class, as a school, and as a district. Talk with administrators and colleagues. (Refer to the section on "The School District" on page 15.)

☐ **2** Examine the cumulative record folders for each student or randomly selected students, depending upon the number of students/classes you teach.

> ▶ Make a list of students' names, if possible.

- Look for information about the family/home situation. Note names of parents/guardians. Don't assume these people have the same last name as the student.
- Note any outstanding strengths, weaknesses, interests, and talents—both academic and nonacademic.
- Notice whether students were enrolled in any special programs for learning disabilities, speech therapy, gifted education, and so on.
- Make note of any chronic health problems, including allergies.
- Determine whether there are any students who, for religious reasons (a) cannot participate in some school activities or have some restrictions on them; or (b) will participate in some religious holidays or activities that other children won't, such as Yom Kippur and Passover (Jewish) or Ramadan (Muslim).
- Look for unique characteristics of your students such as language differences, socioeconomic status, or at-risk indicators that may require special attention when planning for instruction.

☐ **3** Keep an open mind about the students as you read their folders. Try not to let negative or unusual information lead to negative opinions about students. Use all information to help you design instruction that recognizes each student's strengths, background, and personal learning needs.

☐ **4** Estimate the academic range, mean, and composition of the class. Use this data to tentatively answer questions such as:

- Is the group about average in reading (math, spelling, and so on)?
- Is there a larger than expected number of high or low achievers? What adaptations might be needed to address this range of ability levels?
- Will grade-level texts and supplementary materials be appropriate?

check ✓ when completed

> ▶ Are there any students with disabilities who require special consideration?

☐ **5** Prepare a file folder for each student in which you store room records, work samples, and other information throughout the year. (Some teachers have each student design their own folder during the first few days of school.)

# MAKING MANAGEMENT PREPARATIONS

Even before creating lesson plans, consider a number of non-instructional issues that will help you manage the students and the classroom environment. These issues include organizing instructional materials, classroom helpers, class lists and rosters, home-school communication, birthdays and other celebrations, and distributing textbooks.

Even though none of these issues directly relates to instruction, each needs your attention. Thinking about these issues prior to the start of school will help create a more orderly classroom and promote a smooth transition in the opening days of the school year.

Check ✓
when
completed

# Organizing Materials

☐ **1** Establish a filing system for your instructional plans, notes, and student handouts and tests. A separate file folder can be created for each course unit to hold pertinent notes and resource materials.

☐ **2** Set up a filing system for storing district and school communications.

☐ **3** Store supplementary materials on shelves, in boxes, or in file drawers according to curricular areas.

# Classroom Helpers

☐ **1** Determine whether you want student helpers. If so, determine what tasks students can be responsible for, how you will select helpers, and how long a student will hold a particular job. Have a job chart ready on the first day. Consider tasks such as:

- ▶ Attendance recorder
- ▶ Lunch count recorder
- ▶ Line leader
- ▶ Light switcher
- ▶ Classroom librarian
- ▶ Plant waterer
- ▶ Playground-equipment manager
- ▶ Pet tenders

☐ **2** Determine how classroom helper assignments will be rotated to provide all students an opportunity to help. Roles are often held one or two weeks before assignments are rotated.

☐ **3** Secondary school student aides are sometimes available for a single class period or for an ongoing regular time. Create a contract that lists possible duties (e.g., filing, grading, recording grades, attendance, computer work, errands) and expectations (e.g., privacy, confidentiality, promptness, accuracy,

*check ✓ when completed*

dependability).

☐ **4** Determine whether you want to use adult helpers such as paraeducators or volunteer parents. If so, decide what roles they may serve and determine guidelines and expectations for them. Consult your principal or mentor teacher for suggestions.

## Class Lists and Rosters

☐ **1** Prepare a class roster that has a place for student names on the left and six or eight blank columns on the right. Make several copies to use for recording items such as:

- ▶ Textbook checkout
- ▶ Assignments
- ▶ Skills mastery
- ▶ Book orders
- ▶ Field trip permission slips
- ▶ Phone calls made to parents

☐ **2** Don't record names and other information in your grade book for at least one full week; some students may be switched to other rooms and/or transfer students may enter school several days late.

☐ **3** Consider preparing a student profile card with information such as: name, names of parents/guardians, home address, work and home phone, birth date, bus route, any special needs, and any regular medications taken. Include any activity (e.g., sports, drama) that may cause the student to miss class. You might also ask them to include important or interesting personal information they wish to share. Students can fill out their own cards. This is particularly good for new students for whom data may not be available from the office.

# School-Home Communication

☐ **1** Prepare materials to send home with the students on the first day (letter to parents, classroom rules, and student profile cards).

☐ **2** Consider preparing an introductory letter for parents/guardians. This letter could be sent home with students during their first week of school or distributed at a Back-To-School Night if your school has one. Don't overwhelm parents/ guardians; keep the letter brief. Make the letter specific to your room. The letter might include:

- ▶ Something about your background
- ▶ Some information about the content for the year and your approach to instruction
- ▶ A brief explanation of your assessment/grading system
- ▶ Your policy on homework
- ▶ Supplies needed
- ▶ An invitation for parents/guardians to share their information or skills with your pupils, when and if appropriate
- ▶ An open invitation for parents/guardians to visit your classroom
- ▶ Your sincere desire for good school-home communication throughout the year
- ▶ The school phone number and your extension, and possibly your home phone number and your email address.

☐ **3** If your school has an Open House or Back-To-School Night, consider what you want to share. This may include much of the information in the previous item, but also a syllabus, an overview of the curriculum, your instructional strategies, an assessment procedure, and academic and behavioral expectations.

check ✓ when completed

# Birthdays and Other Celebrations

☐ **1** Decide whether you want to celebrate birthdays in your classroom. Primary students and, to a lesser degree, intermediate grade students like this recognition.

☐ **2** Consider creating a monthly calendar with birthdays and possibly other information on it.

☐ **3** Decide when to celebrate birthdays that fall on weekends or holidays or during the summer.

- ▶ Weekend and holiday birthdays could be celebrated the following school day.
- ▶ Summer birthdays could be celebrated on one's "six-month" birthday.

☐ **4** Plan how you want to celebrate birthdays.

- ▶ Consult your principal or school handbook on party policies, including refreshments.
- ▶ Determine whether you want to present each child with a small gift, such as a pencil or bookmark. If so, purchase the objects now, in bulk.
- ▶ Determine whether you want to grant special birthday privileges, such as being first in line all day, getting to choose a book for shared reading, sharing special snacks from home, and so on.

☐ **5** Most schools have specific policies for celebrating certain holidays, such as Halloween, Christmas, Hanukkah, Martin Luther King, Jr. Day, Easter, and Passover. Inquire now about these policies, so that you understand what is expected.

# Use of Instructional Resources

☐ **1** Decide when to distribute textbooks. Because the first day of school often includes announcements and activities, you might want to wait until the second or third day, or even just before the first time they are used.

☐ **2** Decide how to efficiently distribute the textbooks.
- ▶ Use an inventory form to record the book number and the student's name.
- ▶ Decide on a procedure to distribute the books (e.g., students come up one row at a time, then you record the book number and student's name).

☐ **3** Think about how to inform your students about the use of classroom instructional resources such as computers and printers, lab equipment, machinery/tools, and other materials.

☐ **4** If your school requires that students use a planner, think about how you will introduce it to your students.

# DETERMINING PROCEDURES AND RULES

Classroom discipline is an important concern of all teachers, and effective use of classroom procedures and rules can minimize the chance for student misbehavior.

**PROCEDURES** are approved ways to help students accomplish specific tasks. Procedures increase the shared understanding for an activity between you and the students, reduce the complexity of the classroom environment to a predictable structure, and allow for efficient use of time. Before school starts, think about aspects of your classroom when you want a standard way for students to complete a task, and then decide the exact procedure you want the students to follow.

**RULES** are general behavioral standards or expectations used to regulate individual behavior and to avoid disruptive behavior. It is important to decide ahead of time, before school starts, what your plan will be to deal with misbehavior.

When students misbehave, you must be ready to deliver appropriate consequences to get them back on task. Give careful attention to the rules you would like to have in your classroom and the consequences that you will deliver if students follow or break the rules.

check ✓ when completed

# Classroom Procedures

☐ **1** Formulate several positive and up-beat ways to begin and end the day/class period.

☐ **2** Decide on procedures to use in certain areas of your classroom, such as:
- ▶ Student desks and storage areas for belongings
- ▶ Storage for class materials used by all students
- ▶ Pencil sharpener, waste basket
- ▶ Computer areas, learning stations, equipment areas

☐ **3** Decide on procedures for students entering or leaving the classroom
- ▶ Beginning and ending of the day
- ▶ Leaving the room
- ▶ Returning to the room

☐ **4** Decide on out-of-room procedures that are consistent with school policies
- ▶ Hall passes to leave the room
- ▶ Lockers
- ▶ Cafeteria
- ▶ Playground

☐ **5** Decide on procedures for activities and seatwork
- ▶ Signals for student attention
- ▶ Student movement in and out of any groups
- ▶ Distributing books, supplies, and materials
- ▶ Requesting help from the teacher
- ▶ Gathering and returning assignments

☐ **6** Decide on procedures to begin the day/class period.
- ▶ Taking attendance and lunch count
- ▶ Late students
- ▶ Expected student behavior during this opening time

check ✓ when completed

☐ **7** Plan some method for collecting students' assignments. Ask your mentor or a colleague for advice.

- ▶ Designate one basket where students can place completed work.
- ▶ In an open area, place individual baskets, folders, large envelopes, or mailboxes made from cardboard boxes (one per child) where students can store notes to parents, assessed work, and any other materials that should go home at the end of the day.
- ▶ If students change classes hourly, design a system accordingly (e.g., separate baskets or different colored folders for each hourly class).

☐ **8** Decide how you want to have students label their papers (name, date, and class period) and how you want them to turn papers in (e.g. a tray or basket).

☐ **9** Determine how you will have your students keep track of assignments, due dates, and other obligations. Consider planners, homework assignments sheets, or other approaches.

# Rules

☐ **1** Check with your principal, grade-level team, or department to see whether there is a common discipline policy to be used in each classroom.

☐ **2** If your school does not have a common discipline policy, formulate a few concise rules for expected behavior in your classroom. Tell students what you want from them, even if it sounds obvious to you.

- ▶ Choose only rules you can't live without and are willing to enforce consistently.
- ▶ Consider having students help you identify the rules so they feel part of the process.
- ▶ State rules positively, e.g.:
  - ▶ Follow the teacher's directions.
  - ▶ Raise your hand and wait to be recognized.

Check ✓ when completed

- Keep your hands, feet, and objects to yourself.

☐ **3** Discuss the rationale for the rules with the students to ensure they understand and see the need for each rule.

☐ **4** Consider writing these rules on a poster for display and discussion on the first day of school.

☐ **5** Plan to state the rules with authority to clearly indicate boundaries for unacceptable behaviors. Be comfortable with your authority, but exercise it only to the degree needed.

☐ **6** Formulate ways to positively reinforce good behavior.

- Consider reinforcers such as inexpensive stickers, awards, or fill-in notes to parents.
- Consult other teachers for reinforcement ideas.
- Set goals or standards and determine what good things will happen when these are followed or met. Plan to discuss these with students.

☐ **7** Decide on a series of responses you will use when students misbehave.

- The consequence should be in proportion to the severity of the misbehavior (e.g., mild responses for mild behavior).
- Consider a series of mild, moderate, and severe responses to misbehavior.
  - Mild responses might include nonverbal responses such as hand signals to give directions, or simply standing near the student.
  - Mild responses might include verbal responses, such as calling on the student during the lesson, using humor, reminding students of the rules, giving the student choices to solve the misbehavior, or giving a reprimand.

*check ✓ when completed*

- ▶ Moderate responses might include loss of privileges, change of seat assignment, written reflections on the problem, time-out, detentions, contacting the parents, or visiting the principal.
- ▶ Severe responses often involve contacting the principal and/or parents and may involve special behavioral contracts with students.

☐ **8** Prepare to be "tested" by at least one student the first day of school. Consult a mentor for suggestions, and visualize responding appropriately.

☐ **9** Consider circumstances when you will need to involve others to address student misbehavior.

☐ **10** For secondary students, include academic and behavioral expectations in your course requirements. Consider having a sheet which the parent/guardian must sign to acknowledge these policies. (See "Preparing a Syllabus and Policy Sheets" on page 45.)

☐ **11** Consult books on classroom management and discipline that are cited in this book's bibliography.

# MAKING INSTRUCTIONAL PREPARATIONS

Research shows that this and the following section, "Planning for the First Day," are the most important sections of this handbook because, more than anything else, they will help determine your year-long classroom success.

It is easy for beginning teachers to fall into the "night-before-trap" in which they ask themselves two hours before bedtime, "What am I going to do in social studies/health/language arts tomorrow?" For novices, teaching can quickly become routine, textbook-shackled, and possibly even disorganized. A crucial chapter may never get finished, important skills may never get mastered, worthwhile learning experiences may get ignored, and the special learning needs of individual students may go unattended. As a result, student learning suffers. And the teacher constantly feels harried, at loose ends, and perplexed.

By giving attention to a number of instructional issues *before* school starts, you will be better organized and prepared for instruction. You can make instructional preparations in your instructional planning, student assessment, syllabus and policy sheets, your grading policy, homework, motivation, back-up activities, and even in gathering materials for a substitute teacher.

Check ✓
when
completed

# Weekly Time Schedules

☐ **1** For elementary classrooms, prepare a weekly time schedule that blocks time for each subject area.

- ▶ Ask your mentor, a colleague, or your principal to help you design a time schedule for your classroom.
- ▶ Include times for special teachers and activities in areas such as physical education, music, art, foreign language, computer lab, and library.
- ▶ Include time for lunch, recesses, and afternoon cleanup.
- ▶ Include regular time, possibly daily, for individual instruction and assistance.
- ▶ Include your planning time.

☐ **2** For middle and secondary classrooms, prepare a chart showing the classes you teach for each class period throughout the week.

☐ **3** Post the weekly schedule in your classroom. Post the class time schedule if students change hourly.

# Long-Range Plans

☐ **1** For each curricular area, use the textbook and related materials to make a week-by-week list of topics you must cover during the first evaluation period. Some districts have curriculum guides that provide this information. A sample outline for middle school language arts may include:

| | |
|---|---|
| Weeks 1 and 2 | Writing a Personal Narrative |
| Week 3 | Improving Sentences |
| Week 4 and 5 | Writing an Explanation |
| Week 6 | Improving Verb Choice |

| Week 7 | Writing a Short Story |
| Week 8 | Open |

❏ **2** Before creating lesson plans, use this week-by-week schedule to prepare a day-to-day skeleton plan such as those shown on pages 41 and 42.

❏ **3** In formulating these rough schedules, consider the following:

- ▶ Before doing too much, solicit advice from other teachers, particularly those who teach your same grade level or subject area.

- ▶ Take into account your school's annual yearly progress with No Child Left Behind. Consult others as necessary and make adjustments in your long-range plans.

- ▶ If it makes no difference where the topics fall in the school year, assign the topics you consider most important or most "teachable" early enough in the year so that you won't omit or slight them as time runs out. Note, however, that some topics are built upon previous ones and this prerequisite information must be covered first.

- ▶ In elementary schools, look for ways to integrate subjects. For example, if studying folktales in reading, consider writing them in language arts and also reading pertinent ones in social studies.

- ▶ Take grading periods, holidays, and staff development days into consideration as you prepare long-range plans.

- ▶ Examine the curriculum for the previous grade to see how it might affect your long-range schedule.

- ▶ Be careful not to "overschedule" yourself. Leave some time for review near the end of each unit or chapter, for re-instruction if skills weren't mastered the first time, and for any unexcused occurrences, such as school closings due to inclement weather.

- ▶ Allow yourself some flexibility. Don't expect these to be rigid plans.

# Skeleton, Long-Range Plan for Third Grade Social Studies
## *(First nine weeks)*

**Three Days Per Week—Monday, Wednesday, Friday**

| | |
|---|---|
| September 6 | Introduction; overview |
| September 8 | Map/globe review game |
| September 11 | Chapter 1—Living in Communities*—Introduction |
| September 13 | Write Chamber of Commerce for information |
| September 15 | Lesson 1—Different Communities |
| September 18 | " |
| September 20 | What we know about our community |
| September 22 | " |
| September 25 | Write letters to pen pal school |
| September 27 | " |
| September 29 | Open |
| October 2 | Chapter 2—Communities and Geography—Introduction |
| October 4 | Lesson 1—Geography of the U.S.A.—Introduction |
| October 6 | Lesson 1—Video of U.S. geography |
| October 9 | Lesson 1—Map work |
| October 11 | Columbus Day** |
| October 13 | Open |
| October 16 | Lesson 2—Caring for the Environment—Introduction |
| October 18 | Pollution |
| October 20 | Recycling |
| October 23 | Role of local zoo (zoo resource person?) |
| October 25 | Trip to zoo? |
| October 27 | Open |
| October 30 | Halloween** |
| November 1 | Lesson 3—Citizenship in our community (voting) |
| November 3 | Summarize/review Chapters 1 and 2 |

\* Textbook has too many good ideas for all to be implemented. Select only the best.

\*\*Will study Columbus and Halloween rather than the topic from the unit.

# Skeleton, Long-Range Plan for High School Biology
## *(First eight weeks)*

| | |
|---|---|
| August 25 | Introduction; Biology Brain Teaser |
| August 26 | Chapter 1—Investigating Life |
| August 27 | " |
| August 30 | Chapter 2—What Is "Life"? |
| August 31 | " |
| September 1 | " |
| September 2 | Chapter 3—Diversity of Life |
| September 3 | " |
| September 6 | No School; Labor Day |
| September 7 | Chapter 4—The Beginning of Life |
| September 8 | " |
| September 9 | " |
| September 10 | Open |
| September 13 | Chapter 5—Cell Structure and Function |
| September 14 | " |
| September 15 | " |
| September 16 | " |
| September 17 | Computer Simulation |
| September 20 | Chapter 5—Review? Test? |
| September 21 | Chapter 6—Plants |
| September 22 | " |
| September 23 | " |
| September 24 | Open |
| September 27 | Chapter 7—Animals |
| September 28 | " |
| September 29 | " |
| September 30 | " |
| October 1 | Chapters 5, 6, and 7—Review? Test? Computer Simulation? |
| October 4 | Open |
| October 5 | Open |
| October 6 | Chapter 8—Neither Plant nor Animal |
| October 7 | " |
| October 8 | No School—Inservice Day |
| October 11 | Chapters 1-8 Summary/Review |
| October 12 | Chapter 9—Microbes |
| October 13 | " |
| October 14 | " |
| October 15 | Open |

## Motivating Your Students

☐ **1** Read one or more books on motivating students that are listed in the bibliography of this book on page 71.

☐ **2** As you begin thinking about how you will plan lessons, build in the following motivational principles:

- ▶ Intent—arouse the students' curiosity
- ▶ Relevance—relate instruction to the students' personal needs and goals
- ▶ Expectancy—help the students see that they can be successful in each activity
- ▶ Satisfaction—help the students see what they have accomplished

☐ **3** Vary your instructional approach within each lesson. Consider ways to vary student grouping, activities, materials, tasks, and assignments.

☐ **4** Frequently have students actively engaged in instructional activities. For example, consider hands-on activities, cooperative learning, discussion, and group projects.

## Preparing for Lesson Planning

☐ **1** Start a file folder for each major topic in your long-range plans. Into it, put notes and ideas about how to teach this topic. Use these as the basis for future lesson plans. For example, consider hands-on activities, cooperative learning, discussion, and group projects. Notes and materials in these content file folders may include:

- ▶ Whole-class, group, and individual activities
- ▶ Possible instructional materials
- ▶ Ways to introduce or conclude topics or units
- ▶ Assignments/projects/learning experiences

*check ✓ when completed*

- Resource people, field trips, etc.
- Bulletin boards
- Assessment ideas
- Possible curricular integration
- Appropriate homework

☐ **2** Consider asking a mentor/colleague for feedback and suggestions.

☐ **3** Consider the unique characteristics of your students and plan to differentiate your instruction for all learners. Take into account factors such as:

- Academic ability
- Exceptionalities
- Language
- Socioeconomic status

☐ **4** Plan for ways to integrate technology into your instruction.

## Daily Lesson Plans

☐ **1** Expand your skeleton plan and topic/unit folders for the first week of school into daily lesson plans. Keep these pointers in mind:

- For each lesson plan, specify objectives, instructional activities and tasks, and the means of assessment.
- You may want to keep instruction rather traditional until you are confident you have established adequate student control.
- Keep all lessons within the set time limits in your weekly time schedule.

☐ **2** Record your lesson plans in the format that may be required by your school.

☐ **3** Because most beginning teachers are required to submit their lesson plans to the principal for review prior to instruction, lesson plans often need to be prepared about a week ahead.

*check ✓ when completed*

☐ **4** When planning, ponder how to manage and even minimize paperwork. There are so many first-week demands that you don't want to be swamped by grading papers.

☐ **5** Consider designing assessment tools such as rubrics and tests before beginning to plan daily lessons—this will help you stay focused on the objectives as you plan content, activities, and instructional tasks.

☐ **6** Use assessment information to inform your instructional planning. In particular, this will help guide your selection of content.

☐ **7** Always overplan so you don't have open time at the end of class, especially for the first week or two. (See "Back-Up Activities" on page 49.)

# Preparing a Syllabus and Policy Sheets

☐ **1** For elementary grades, think about how to tell students the content of each subject area, instructional approaches, and grading procedures.

☐ **2** At the middle and high school levels, consider giving students a course syllabus with this introductory information.

> ▶ A course syllabus includes the course title, the title of the textbook, a brief course description, course objectives, a content outline, course requirements, how grades will be calculated, the homework policy, the attendance and tardiness policy, and a listing of the classroom rules and procedures.

☐ **3** Some teachers prefer to have the rules, procedures, and classroom policies in a policy sheet that is separate from the course syllabus.

☐ **4** Because the first day at many schools is not a full day, many teachers postpone distributing the syllabus until the next day. See "Conducting the First Day" on page 54.

# Tentative Student Assessment

☐ **1** Prepare some procedures to help you tentatively estimate the students' achievement in major subject areas such as mathematics, spelling, handwriting, written composition, reading, or other areas where prior knowledge or achievement is important. Assessment procedures might include:

- ▶ Pre-tests
- ▶ Review lessons
- ▶ Worksheets
- ▶ Oral activities
- ▶ Observation checklists
- ▶ Work samples

☐ **2** These assessments will be most practical and valid if they are an integral part of instruction rather than unrelated "tests." That is, spelling and handwriting could be assessed via a review spelling test or a written paragraph, math by problems worked at the blackboard, reading by student oral reading during an assigned selection, etc.

☐ **3** Use the class rosters you made (see page 26) to record the results of your assessment. Use a simple coding system such as:

- \+ = Above Average
- 0 = Average
- − = Below Average
- ▶ Compare your assessment data with information in the students' cumulative record folders. Consider discussing any major discrepancies or questions with other teachers.
- ▶ Begin thinking how you can make use of this information in constructing lesson plans, assignments, and instructional groups.

*Check ✓ when completed*

☐ **4** Plan to assess your students' prior knowledge about each unit you plan to teach. Use this initial assessment to guide your unit and lesson planning.

# Determining Your Grading Policy

☐ **1** Consult your school's reporting system before determining your grading policy. You must match your assessment practices and grading system to the school's reporting system.

☐ **2** Decide on the ways that you will assess student learning—homework, tests, projects, etc.

☐ **3** Determine the relative weight each assessment approach will carry when you prepare report card grades (e.g., 30% homework, 30% tests, 20% projects, 20% seatwork)

☐ **4** Decide whether to have points, percentages, or letter grades for assessment. All have pros and cons. Discuss this with your mentor and/or colleagues.

☐ **5** Plan to inform your students of your grading policy.

☐ **6** Decide how to record information in your gradebook for student achievement, attendance, and conduct. Some schools have computer programs for the gradebook.

☐ **7** Have professional yet realistic standards/expectations in assignments, homework, assessment, and grading. Discuss with your mentor and/or colleagues.

# Planning for Homework

☐ **1** Learn whether your school has a homework policy.

☐ **2** Determine the purpose of homework in your class and how it will enhance student learning.

- Decide whether homework will be used to review content previously covered, to examine new content, or a combination.
- Select an appropriate amount and frequency of homework for the grade level. Talk to other teachers at your grade level to get a perspective about what is reasonable.
- Do not use homework as punishment.

☐ **3** Determine how homework will fit into your assessment system. (See "Determining Your Grading Policy" on page 47.)

☐ **4** Provide students with guidelines for when and how to complete homework.

- Designate an area of the chalkboard for displaying all homework assignments and due dates.
- Include time in your lesson plans to discuss your homework procedures with the students.

☐ **5** Select a process for providing feedback and grading homework.

- Determine ways you will evaluate the homework.
- Determine how you will handle late work.
- Determine consequences if work is not turned in. Discuss this with a mentor or colleague.

☐ **6** Formulate a way of assessing daily work that is compatible with the district assessment system (which may include a specific grading system, specially designed report cards, portfolios, and so on).

- First, find out what other teachers do.
- Then decide what will be assessed—all daily work or just selected work.

☐ **7** Again, consider how to manage paperwork rather than having it manage you.

Check ✓
when
completed

# Back-Up Activities

☐ **1** Prepare some brief educational activities to use when plans don't take as long as expected, when children finish early, or at the end of the day. Place descriptions of these activities and related materials in a card file or a folder.

☐ **2** These backup activities can be anything from a teacher sharing a story or poem to finding locations on a map to discussing current events. Or they may include brainteasers, educational games, or other fun activities.

# Opening Class Routine

☐ **1** Decide whether you want to have a particular routine to start each class.

☐ **2** Decide how to take attendance, make announcements, and attend to other tasks at the start of the class period.

> ▶ Some teachers have students work on problems, questions, or vocabulary words while they take care of the other administrative tasks.

> ▶ Many elementary school teachers use this time for student helpers to take attendance, water plants, check in classroom library books, etc.

# Folder for Substitute Teachers

☐ **1** Start a folder for substitute teachers. Include at least the following:

> ▶ Standard daily schedule, including the names of special teachers (art, music, physical education, library, and so on)

check ✓ when completed

- Seating chart or class roster with comments about students with special needs
- A copy of classroom rules, procedures, and expectations
- Information about taking attendance and lunch count
- A list of reliable students who can be called on for assistance.
- The name of a nearby teacher to contact if needed or if they have questions
- Names of students who leave the room to go to special classes (e.g., learning disabilities classes, instrumental music, speech therapy) and when they should leave and return
- Names of any aides or paraprofessionals and a description of their general responsibilities
- Several appropriate activity sheets that could be reproduced quickly and used for seatwork
- Location of the backup activities folder
- Include several attendance slips, lunch count sheets, hall passes, and discipline referrals so the substitute teacher doesn't have to search for these.

**Note:** Before school starts, you may not be able to obtain all the information you need to complete this folder. However, begin the folder now.

A successful first day of school takes a lot of preparation. You can't tell students about everything on the first day so you'll need to decide exactly which information to convey on the first day and which on subsequent days.

But you also need to be concerned about how you interact with students and how you establish and enforce behavioral expectations. Therefore, this section begins with some principles to consider when planning for the first day, followed by actions you could take when you actually conduct the first day of school.

# PLANNING FOR THE FIRST DAY

Check ✓
when
completed

# Planning the First Day

Take these planning principles into account as you plan for the first day.

❏ **1** Many schools have shortened periods/days the first day of school. Overplan but don't rush, hurry, or cram in too much.

❏ **2** Keep a whole-class focus because one large group is often easier to monitor than several small groups.

❏ **3** Consider some kind of brief get-acquainted activity, either for the first day or subsequent days.

❏ **4** Teach something the first day. Have students do some kind of schoolwork, particularly something that can be sent home. (Emphasize to students to share their work with parents.) Select first-day activities where all or most students can succeed.

❏ **5** Plan uncomplicated lessons to help students be successful.

❏ **6** Organize the flow of lesson activities to keep things moving.

- ▶ Get students quickly prepared for the lesson.
- ▶ Maintain momentum and provide signals for the change of activities.
- ▶ Minimize confusion during the transition between activities by stating clear expectations for what you want the students to do during the transition time.

❏ **7** Maintain student attention.

- ▶ Get the active attention of all students before starting a lesson.
- ▶ Monitor students for signs of confusion or inattention.

❏ **8** Plan to clearly state your rules, procedures, and academic expectations.

❏ **9** Closely monitor student compliance with rules

*check ✓ when completed*

and procedures, and provide corrective feedback.

☐ **10** Stop inappropriate behavior quickly.

☐ **11** Be available, visible, and in charge. Move around the room.

☐ **12** If you are teaching elementary students:

- ▶ Plan short lessons—not full-period ones. Follow each by a brief discussion of rules and procedures.
- ▶ Select your first read-aloud book, preferably short, self-contained, and humorous.

## Conducting the First Day

☐ **1** Use the sequence of topics listed here flexibly; feel free to re-arrange items to fit your situation.

☐ **2** Greet the students.

- ▶ Stand by the door before class begins.
- ▶ Welcome students as they enter.

☐ **3** Tell students about their seat assignments.

- ▶ If assigning seats, have students' names on the desks or have a transparency showing where their seats are located.

☐ **4** Handle administrative tasks.

☐ **5** Take attendance and lunch count.

- ▶ Devise an easy, quick way to handle these tasks.

☐ **6** Make introductions.

- ▶ Tell students about yourself, personally and professionally.
- ▶ Consider some get-acquainted activity to have students introduce themselves.

☐ **7** Introduce the course.

- ▶ Describe the topics of study.

- ▶ Describe typical instructional activities.
- ▶ Show the textbooks.

☐ **8** Present course requirements.

- ▶ If you have prepared a course syllabus, distribute and go over it.
- ▶ Discuss course content, instructional activities, and the means of assessing student performance.

☐ **9** Discuss classroom rules and procedures.

- ▶ Post the rules or have students help formulate several most important ones.
- ▶ Discuss the rules and procedures and the reasons for having them.

☐ **10** Conduct an initial activity.

- ▶ Have an interesting, easy activity to deal with some content, possibly review material.

☐ **11** End the class period.

- ▶ Be sure to remind students about homework or other assignments.
- ▶ Establish a daily routine to end the class period, allowing students time to put papers and supplies away, clean up the work areas, and gather their belongings if they will be leaving the classroom.

# ORGANIZING YOUR CLASSROOM AND MATERIALS

After you have become acquainted with the district and school, made management and instructional preparations, decided on procedures and rules, and planned for your first day, then you are ready to prepare the physical layout of your classroom.

Think about the type of classroom environment you would like to create. Your decision about the arrangement of student desks, for example, will be influenced by the type of interaction you want to occur among students. When decorating the room with posters and displays, give attention to function as well as aesthetics.

Your decisions about your classroom and materials will include room identification, desk arrangements, seat selection and nametags, room arrangement, and room decoration.

## Room Identification

☐ **1** Post your name, class level, and room number outside your classroom door where students can see them the first day of school. For secondary classes, post your name and class schedule for each hour outside the door.

☐ **2** Plan to write some welcoming statement on the chalkboard, such as "Welcome, I'm glad you're here."

## Desk Arrangements

☐ **1** Decide how to arrange the students' desks (rows, clusters of four desks, U-shaped arrangement, etc.). You may want to consider using traditional rows for the first few weeks. Experienced teachers say this layout leads to the fewest discipline problems.

☐ **2** While deciding upon room arrangement, visualize yourself teaching the class in a variety of situations. What works? What is questionable?

## Seat Selection and Name Tags

☐ **1** Decide whether you will let students choose their seats or whether you will assign the seats. If the latter, write a seating chart in pencil.

☐ **2** Consider whether you want name tags affixed to student desks. For classes that change hourly, note cards folded in half with a student's name on one side may be satisfactory. Or prepare a seating chart on a transparency for each hourly class.

☐ **3** For young bus riders, put the bus number on the tags.

check ✓ when completed

# Room Arrangement

☐ **1** Determine your room arrangement. Include:
  ▶ Location of teacher's desk
  ▶ Location of additional furniture, such as file cabinets, display tables, and tables for small-group work
  ▶ Location of teacher supplies and student supplies
  ▶ Computer area
  ▶ Location of other areas, such as an independent reading center, an art corner, science center, etc.

☐ **2** Ask the school secretary about any extra furniture you may want, such as a table for reading groups or science displays, a plant stand, bookcases, a portable chalkboard, and a wheeled cart. Obtain any that are available.

# Room Decoration

☐ **1** Prepare colorful, attractive bulletin boards.
  ▶ Keep them simple and inexpensive. Use what is available, and check about available school or PTA funds for what you buy.
  ▶ Make bulletin boards functional, not merely decorative. They should solicit student input and relate to material that will be covered the first couple of weeks.
  ▶ Consider ways to lessen the load of preparing bulletin boards by having groups of students take turns preparing one.
  ▶ Consider decorating one bulletin board or wall space with only a border and a title on which you can immediately display students' work.

- ▶ Devote one display area to introducing your students to one another. Title the bulletin board "Who's Who?" On the first day of school, have students make nametags that are posted there.

❏ **2** Decide where to post notices and other information (e.g., class schedule, calendar, homework assignments and due dates, etc.). Prepare these and post them.

❏ **3** Display any pertinent pictures, posters, charts, and maps.

❏ **4** Don't overdecorate. Many elementary school classrooms have so much on the walls that students are overwhelmed. As the year progresses, remove some items and put up new ones.

❏ **5** Keep room decoration in perspective; don't let it take too much of your time. Instructional and management planning are far more important than room decoration.

# THE FINAL CHECK

The big day is upon you. All of your earlier preparations should give you a feeling of confidence that you are prepared for the first day of school. Yet it is natural to still wonder how it will turn out and to be somewhat nervous about meeting the students for the first time.

You will be better prepared and feel more confident about your first day if you have a number of materials ready. And finally, you may want to assess your preparation in a number of areas. Give any areas that need work special attention in the opening weeks of the school year.

If you believe you'd benefit from additional suggestions about the rest of your first year of teaching, consult one or more of the publications in the bibliography section "Beginning the School Year," on page 68.

Check ✓
when
completed

# HAVE THESE MATERIALS READY

❑ **1** Your name, class level, and room number are posted outside the classroom.

❑ **2** Nametags are affixed to desks, or materials are set up for students to make their own nametags, or directions are displayed to tell students where to sit.

❑ **3** Your name and the daily/weekly schedule are posted in the room.

❑ **4** Room displays are attractive and welcoming.

❑ **5** You have enough books and school supplies for every student.

❑ **6** Your lesson plans for the first week of school are on your desk.

❑ **7** A complete class roster is on your desk.

❑ **8** All teaching materials for the first day's lessons are ready for use.

# FINAL CHECK!

Shortly before school starts, assess your preparation in the following areas. Give special attention to areas that need work in the opening weeks of the school year.

|  | Needs Work | O.K. | Excellent |
|---|---|---|---|
| 1. Instructional materials | 1 | 2 | 3 |
| 2. Physical environment | 1 | 2 | 3 |
| 3. Knowledge of students | 1 | 2 | 3 |
| 4. Management skills | 1 | 2 | 3 |
| 5. First several days of lesson plans | 1 | 2 | 3 |
| 6. Long-range plans | 1 | 2 | 3 |
| 7. Assessment procedures | 1 | 2 | 3 |
| 8. Acquaintance with staff, including mentor | 1 | 2 | 3 |
| 9. Familiarity with district/school rules | 1 | 2 | 3 |
| 10. Self-confidence | 1 | 2 | 3 |

Relax, look forward to today—and the rest of the year! And reward yourself in some way at the end of the first day or week for a job well begun.

# Bibliography for Classroom Management and Related Issues

BIBLIOGRAPHY

# Beginning the School Year

## K-12

Guillaume, Andrea M. (2004). *K-12 classroom teaching: A primer for new professionals* (2nd ed.). Upper Saddle River, NJ: Prentice-Hall/Merrill. 239 pages. Provides a very practical overview to many aspects to teaching, including issues needing attention at the start of the school year.

Kronowitz, Ellen L. (2004). *Your first year of teaching and beyond* (4th ed.). Boston: Allyn & Bacon. 250 pages. Addresses many aspects of teaching with chapters on topics such as classroom organization and management, discipline, parents, materials, curriculum planning, and the first day.

Partin, Ronald L. (2004). *Classroom survival guide: Practical strategies, management techniques, and reproducibles for new and experienced teachers* (2nd ed.). San Francisco: Jossey-Bass. 400 pages. Provides practical tips on many aspects of organizing and managing a classroom. Addresses creating a supportive learning environment, creating successful lesson, alternatives to lectures, effective use of time, and more.

Thompson, Julia G. (2002). *First-year teacher's survival kit*. San Francisco: Jossey-Bass. 485 pages. Provides an excellent, thorough, yet practical guide to all aspects of starting your school year. Many useful charts and specific guides. Covers planning for behavior, curriculum, and instruction.

Wong, Harry K., & Wong, Rosemary T. (2004). The first days of school: How to be an effective teacher (3rd ed.). Mountain View, CA: Harry Wong Publications. 352 pages. Is a highly popular guide for beginning teachers. Loaded with very practical guidelines on positive expectations, classroom management, lesson mastery, and other vital topics.

## Elementary

Bosch, Karen A., & Kersey, Katharine C. (2000). *The first-year teacher: Teaching with confidence (K-8)* (2nd ed.). Washington, DC: National Education Association. 168

pages. Includes five chapters on getting started, working with parents, time management, and ending the year.

Jonson, Kathleen F. (2002). *The new elementary teacher's handbook: Flourishing in your first year* (2nd ed.). Thousand Oaks, CA: Corwin Press. 231 pages. Provides thorough, practical advise on topics such as organizing the classroom, classroom management, preparing instructional plans, dealing with discipline, assessing student work, and working with parents.

Murray, Bonnie P. (2002). *The new teacher's complete sourcebook: Grades K-4*. New York: Scholastic Professional Books. 192 pages. Is packed with tips on topics such as setting up your classroom, preparing lessons, determining your classroom management system, managing paperwork, and working with parents.

Terry, Alice. (1997). *Every teacher's guide to classroom management*. Cypress, CA: Creative Teaching Press, Inc. 144 pages. Offers many practical suggestions for managing time, people, space, materials, and paperwork.

Thompson, Ellen A. (2001). *I teach first grade: A treasure chest of teaching wisdom*. Peterborough, NH: Crystal Springs Books. 240 pages. Offers guidance about classroom environment and set-up, classroom routines and management, community building, assessment, curriculum, thematic instruction, and parents.

### *Middle and Secondary*

Arnold, Harriett. (2001). *Succeeding in the secondary classroom: Strategies for middle and high school teachers*. Thousand Oaks, CA: Corwin Press. 134 pages. Provides practical suggestions for preparing for the first day, instructional planning, record keeping, classroom management and discipline, and working with colleagues and parents.

Cushman, Kathleen. (2003). *Fires in the bathroom: Advice for teachers from high school students*. New York: The New Press. 204 pages. Provides guidance about topics such as knowing your students, respect and fairness, classroom behavior, creating a culture of success, motivation, teaching difficult academic work, and what to do when things go wrong. Based on the candid discussions and recommendations from a number of urban high school students.

Kottler, Ellen; Kottler, Jeffrey A.; & Kottler, Cary J. (2003). *Secrets for secondary school teachers: How to succeed in your first year* (2nd ed.). Thousand Oaks, CA: Corwin Press. 224 pages. Includes 17 chapters on topics such as becoming acquainted to the school, organizing the classroom, dressing, the first day, paperwork, lunch, connecting with students, communicating with parents, and dealing with stress.

Lindberg, Jill A., Kelley, Dianne E., & Swick, April M. (2004). *Common-sense classroom management for middle and high school teachers*. Thousand Oaks, CA: Corwin Press. 128 pages. Includes many specific suggestions on organization, planning, classroom atmosphere, discipline, and instruction.

Wyatt, Robert L., & White, J. Elaine. (2002). *Making your first year a success: The secondary teacher's survival guide.* Thousand Oaks, CA: Corwin Press. 120 pages. Is a brief guidebook with suggestions about issues such as starting the school year, classroom management, lesson plans, assessment, and working with parents.

# Classroom Management and Discipline

Burden, Paul R. (2006). *Classroom management: Creating a successful K-12 learning community* (3rd ed.). New York: Wiley & Sons. 277 pages. (for grades K-12)

Burke, Kay. (2000). *What do you do with the kid who . . . : Developing cooperation, self-discipline, and responsibility in the classroom* (2nd ed.). Thousand Oaks, CA: Corwin Press. 294 pages. (for grades K-12)

Canter, Lee. (2006). *Lee Canter's classroom management for academic success*. Bloomington, IN: Solution Tree. 277 pages. (for grades K-12)

Long, James D., & Williams, Robert, L. (2005). *Making it till Friday: Your guide to effective classroom management* (5th ed.). Hightstown, NJ: Princeton Book Company. 287 pages. (for grades K-12)

Thompson, Julia G. (1998). *Discipline survival kit for the secondary teacher*. San Francisco: Jossey-Bass. 366 pages. (for grades 7-12)

# Instructional Planning

Burden, Paul R., & Byrd, David M. (2007). *Methods for effective teaching* (4th ed.). Boston: Allyn & Bacon. 400 pages.

Gronlund, Norman E. (2004). *Writing instructional objectives for teaching and assessment* (7th ed.). Upper Saddle River, NJ: Prentice-Hall/Merrill. 136 pages.

Price, Kay M., & Nelson, Karna L. (2007). *Planning effective instruction: Diversity responsive methods and management* (3rd ed.). Belmont, CA: Thomson Wordsworth. 227 pages.

Skowron, Janice. (2006). *Powerful lesson planning: Every teacher's guide to effective instruction* (2nd ed.). Thousand Oaks, CA: Corwin Press. 176 pages.

# Differentiating Your Instruction

Gregory, Gayle H., & Chapman, Carolyn. (2002). *Differentiated instructional strategies: One size doesn't fit all*. Thousand Oaks, CA: Corwin Press. 145 pages.

Gregory, Gayle H. (2006). *Differentiating instruction with style: Aligning teacher and learner intelligences for maximum achievement*. Thousand Oaks, CA: Corwin Press. 184 pages.

Silver, Harvey R., Strong, Richard W., & Perini, Matthew J. (2000). *So each may learn: Integrating learning styles and multiple intelligences*. Alexandria, VA: Association for Supervision and Curriculum Development. 124 pages.

# Motivating Students

Brophy, Jere. (2004). *Motivating students to learn* (2nd ed.). Mahwah, NJ: Lawrence Earlbaum Associates. 432 pages. (for grades K-12)

Burden, Paul R. (2000). *Powerful classroom management*

*strategies: Motivating students to learn*. Thousand Oaks, CA: Corwin Press. 160 pages. (for grades K-12)

## Assessing Student Learning

Gronlund, Norman E. (2006). *Assessment of student achievement* (8th ed.). Boston: Allyn & Bacon. 232 pages.

## Students At Risk

Freiman, Barry B. (2001). *What teachers need to know about children at risk*. New York: McGraw-Hill. 212 pages.

Payne, Ruby K. (2001). *A framework for understanding poverty* (rev. ed.). Highlands, TX: aha! Process, Inc.

Vaughn, Sharon; Bos, Candace S.; & Schumm, Jeanne S. (2003). *Teaching exceptional, diverse, and at-risk students in the general education classroom* (3rd ed.). Boston: Allyn & Bacon. 536 pages.

## Working With Parents

Diffily, Deborah. (2004). *Teachers and families working together*. Boston: Allyn & Bacon. 178 pages.

Hughes, Melissa; Oakes, Kristen; Lenzo, Caroline; & Carpas, Jackie. (2001). *The elementary teacher's guide to conferences and open houses*. Greensboro, NC: Carson-Dellosa Publishing Co. 96 pages.

McEwan, Elaine K. (2005). *How to deal with parents who are angry, troubled, afraid, or just plain crazy* (2nd ed.). Thousand Oaks, CA: Corwin Press. 169 pages.